Francis Frith's
AROUND OXFORD

PHOTOGRAPHIC MEMORIES

Francis Frith's
AROUND OXFORD

◆

Nick Channer

FRITH
BOOK Co

First published in the United Kingdom in 2000 by
Frith Book Company Ltd

Hardback Edition
ISBN 1-85937-096-9

Paperback Edition 2001
ISBN 1-85937-411-5

British Library Cataloguing in Publication Data

Francis Frith's Around Oxford
Nick Channer

Frith Book Company Ltd
Frith's Barn, Teffont,
Salisbury, Wiltshire SP3 5QP
Tel: +44 (0) 1722 716 376
Email: info@francisfrith.co.uk
www.francisfrith.co.uk

Printed and bound in Great Britain

AS WITH ANY HISTORICAL DATABASE THE FRITH ARCHIVE IS CONSTANTLY BEING CORRECTED AND IMPROVED
AND THE PUBLISHERS WOULD WELCOME INFORMATION ON OMISSIONS OR INACCURACIES

CONTENTS

FRANCIS FRITH: *Victorian Pioneer*

FRANCIS FRITH, Victorian founder of the world-famous photographic archive, was a complex and multitudinous man. A devout Quaker and a highly successful Victorian businessman, he was both philosophic by nature and pioneering in outlook.

By 1855 Francis Frith had already established a wholesale grocery business in Liverpool, and sold it for the astonishing sum of £200,000, which is the equivalent today of over £15,000,000. Now a multi-millionaire, he was able to indulge his passion for travel. As a child he had pored over travel books written by early explorers, and his fancy and imagination had been stirred by family holidays to the sublime mountain regions of Wales and Scotland. 'What a land of spirit-stirring and enriching scenes and places!' he had written. He was to return to these scenes of grandeur in later years to 'recapture the thousands of vivid and tender memories', but with a different purpose. Now in his thirties, and captivated by the new science of photography, Frith set out on a series of pioneering journeys to the Nile regions that occupied him from 1856 until 1860.

INTRIGUE AND ADVENTURE

He took with him on his travels a specially-designed wicker carriage that acted as both dark-room and sleeping chamber. These far-flung journeys were packed with intrigue and adventure. In his life story, written when he was sixty-three, Frith tells of being held captive by bandits, and of fighting 'an awful midnight battle to the very point of surrender with a deadly pack of hungry, wild dogs'. Sporting flowing Arab costume, Frith arrived at Akaba by camel seventy years before Lawrence, where he encountered 'desert princes and rival sheikhs, blazing with jewel-hilted swords'.

During these extraordinary adventures he was assiduously exploring the desert regions bordering the Nile and patiently recording the antiquities and peoples with his camera. He was the first photographer to venture beyond the sixth cataract. Africa was still the mysterious 'Dark Continent', and Stanley and Livingstone's historic meeting was a decade into the future. The conditions for picture taking confound belief. He laboured for hours in his wicker dark-room in the sweltering heat of the desert, while the volatile chemicals fizzed dangerously in their trays. Often he was forced to work in remote tombs and caves where conditions were cooler. Back in London he exhibited his photographs and was 'rapturously cheered' by members of the Royal Society. His reputation as a photographer was made overnight. An eminent modern historian has likened their impact on the population of the time to that on our own generation of the first photographs taken on the surface of the moon.

VENTURE OF A LIFE-TIME

Characteristically, Frith quickly spotted the opportunity to create a new business as a specialist publisher of photographs. He lived in an era of immense and sometimes violent change. For the poor in the early part of Victoria's reign work was a drudge and the hours long, and people had precious little free time to enjoy themselves.

Most had no transport other than a cart or gig at their disposal, and had not travelled far beyond the boundaries of their own town or village. However, by the 1870s, the railways had threaded their way across the country, and Bank Holidays and half-day Saturdays had been made obligatory by Act of Parliament. All of a sudden the ordinary working man and his family were able to enjoy days out and see a little more of the world.

With characteristic business acumen, Francis Frith foresaw that these new tourists would enjoy having souvenirs to commemorate their days out. In 1860 he married Mary Ann Rosling and set out with the intention of photographing every city, town and village in Britain. For the next thirty years he travelled the country by train and by pony and trap, producing fine photographs of seaside resorts and beauty spots that were keenly bought by millions of Victorians. These prints were painstakingly pasted into family albums and pored over during the dark nights of winter, rekindling precious memories of summer excursions.

THE RISE OF FRITH & CO

Frith's studio was soon supplying retail shops all over the country. To meet the demand he gathered about him a small team of photographers, and published the work of independent artist-photographers of the calibre of Roger Fenton and Francis Bedford. In order to gain some understanding of the scale of Frith's business one only has to look at the catalogue issued by Frith & Co in 1886: it runs to some 670

pages, listing not only many thousands of views of the British Isles but also many photographs of most European countries, and China, Japan, the USA and Canada – note the sample page shown above from the hand-written *Frith & Co* ledgers detailing pictures taken. By 1890 Frith had created the greatest specialist photographic publishing company in the world, with over 2,000 outlets – more than the combined number that Boots and WH Smith have today! The picture on the right shows the *Frith & Co* display board at Ingleton in the Yorkshire Dales. Beautifully constructed with mahogany frame and gilt inserts, it could display up to a dozen local scenes.

POSTCARD BONANZA

◆

The ever-popular holiday postcard we know today took many years to develop. In 1870 the Post Office issued the first plain cards, with a pre-printed stamp on one face. In 1894 they allowed other publishers' cards to be sent through the mail with an attached adhesive halfpenny stamp. Demand grew rapidly, and in 1895 a new size of postcard was permitted called the court card, but there was little room for illustration. In 1899, a year after Frith's death, a new card measuring 5.5 x 3.5 inches became the standard format, but it was not until 1902 that the divided back came into being, with address and message on one face and a full-size illustration on the other. *Frith & Co* were in the vanguard of postcard development, and Frith's sons Eustace and Cyril continued their father's monumental task, expanding the number of views offered to the public and recording more and more places in Britain, as the coasts and countryside were opened up to mass travel.

Francis Frith died in 1898 at his villa in Cannes, his great project still growing. The archive he created continued in business for another seventy years. By 1970 it contained over a third of a million pictures of 7,000 cities, towns and villages. The massive photographic record Frith has left to us stands as a living monument to a special and very remarkable man.

Frith's Archive: *A Unique Legacy*

FRANCIS FRITH'S legacy to us today is of immense significance and value, for the magnificent archive of evocative photographs he created provides a unique record of change in 7,000 cities, towns and villages throughout Britain over a century and more. Frith and his fellow studio photographers revisited locations many times down the years to update their views, compiling for us an enthralling and colourful pageant of British life and character.

We tend to think of Frith's sepia views of Britain as nostalgic, for most of us use them to conjure up memories of places in our own lives with which we have family associations. It often makes us forget that to Francis Frith they were records of daily life as it was actually being lived in the cities, towns and villages of his day. The Victorian age was one of great and often bewildering change for ordinary people, and though the pictures evoke an impression of slower times, life was as busy and hectic as it is today.

We are fortunate that Frith was a photographer of the people, dedicated to recording the minutiae of everyday life. For it is this sheer wealth of visual data, the painstaking chronicle of changes in dress, transport, street layouts, buildings, housing, engineering and landscape that captivates us so much today. His remarkable images offer us a powerful link with the past and with the lives of our ancestors.

TODAY'S TECHNOLOGY

Computers have now made it possible for Frith's many thousands of images to be accessed almost instantly. In the Frith archive today, each photograph is carefully 'digitised' then stored on a CD Rom. Frith archivists can locate a single photograph amongst thousands within seconds. Views can be catalogued and sorted under a variety of categories of place and content to the immediate benefit of researchers. Inexpensive reference prints can be created for them at the touch of a mouse button, and a wide range of books and other printed materials assembled and published for a wider, more general readership - in the next twelve months over a hundred Frith local history titles will be published! The

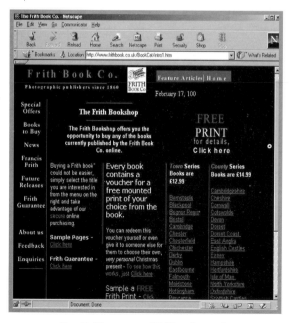

See Frith at www. frithbook.co.uk

day-to-day workings of the archive are very different from how they were in Francis Frith's time: imagine the herculean task of sorting through eleven tons of glass negatives as Frith had to do to locate a particular sequence of pictures! Yet the archive still prides itself on maintaining the same high standards of excellence laid down by Francis Frith, including the painstaking cataloguing and indexing of every view.

It is curious to reflect on how the internet now allows researchers in America and elsewhere greater instant access to the archive than Frith himself ever enjoyed. Many thousands of individual views can be called up on screen within seconds on one of the Frith internet sites, enabling people living continents away to revisit the streets of their ancestral home town, or view places in Britain where they have enjoyed holidays. Many overseas researchers welcome the chance to view special theme selections, such as transport, sports, costume and ancient monuments.

We are certain that Francis Frith would have heartily approved of these modern developments, for he himself was always working at the very limits of Victorian photographic technology.

THE VALUE OF THE ARCHIVE TODAY

Because of the benefits brought by the computer, Frith's images are increasingly studied by social historians, by researchers into genealogy and ancestry, by architects, town planners, and by teachers and schoolchildren involved in local history projects. In addition, the archive offers every one of us a unique opportunity to examine the places where we and our families have lived and worked down the years. Immensely successful in Frith's own era, the archive is now, a century and more on, entering a new phase of popularity.

THE PAST IN TUNE WITH THE FUTURE

Historians consider the Francis Frith Collection to be of prime national importance. It is the only archive of its kind remaining in private ownership and has been valued at a million pounds. However, this figure is now rapidly increasing as digital technology enables more and more people around the world to enjoy its benefits.

Francis Frith's archive is now housed in an historic timber barn in the beautiful village of Teffont in Wiltshire. Its founder would not recognize the archive office as it is today. In place of the many thousands of dusty boxes containing glass plate negatives and an all-pervading odour of photographic chemicals, there are now ranks of computer screens. He would be amazed to watch his images travelling round the world at unimaginable speeds through network and internet lines.

The archive's future is both bright and exciting. Francis Frith, with his unshakeable belief in making photographs available to the greatest number of people, would undoubtedly approve of what is being done today with his lifetime's work. His photographs, depicting our shared past, are now bringing pleasure and enlightenment to millions around the world a century and more after his death.

Around Oxford – *An Introduction*

At the very heart of the county of Oxfordshire lies one of Britain's most beautiful cities. Likened by Thomas Hardy's Jude to 'the heavenly Jerusalem', Oxford's history, beauty and tradition are admired in every corner of the land. As a city it ranks in importance alongside Rome, Athens and Paris, and even when its scholars have left to make their mark on the world, they return again and again to embrace that curiously indefinable 'spirit of Oxford'. In order to see everything that this city has to offer, the visitor, too, would surely have to return again and again - and even when he thinks he has seen every landmark and photographed every tourist attraction, there is always something new and unexpected to stumble upon. A visit to Oxford, 'that sweet city with her dreaming spires', is certain to be a memorable experience.

From the top of Oxford's highest buildings you begin to realise that Oxford, like Florence, another of the world's most beautiful cities, lies at the bottom of a shallow bowl encircled by gentle, protective hills. But why bother with distant vistas when this noble city stretches out below you, its numerous riches waiting to be discovered, photographed and admired?

Oxford has a golden heart - a compact area of less than half a square mile in which the visitor will find a hugely varied assortment of ancient buildings, monuments and treasured landmarks which sit cheek by jowl with houses, shops and offices. In recent years millions of pounds have been spent on the city, restoring and cleaning the stonework of the colleges and university buildings, which had become grimy and black with the inevitable passage of time. Some were even in danger of disintegrating. The utmost care was taken in preserving them; today this great seat of learning, designed by distinguished architects such as Christopher Wren and Nicholas Hawksmoor, looks as good as it did when they helped to create it.

Originally known as Oxnaforda, Oxford was a settlement of some importance long before the University came into being. It began with the foundation of St Frideswide's nunnery in the 8th century. It is first mentioned by name in the Anglo-Saxon Chronicle of 912, which records that King Edward the Elder had made it a fortified frontier position in his defence of Wessex when it was feared that the Danes might attack from the north. The settlement grew, and after the Norman Conquest of 1066, King William appointed his comrade in arms, Robert d'Oilly, to be Oxford's governor. However, it was at the end of the 12th century, when Henry II prevented English clerks from attending the University of Paris, that scholars looked upon Oxford, by now one of the nine most important towns in England, as somewhere suitable to continue their studies. The first group may have been joined by others from Paris, as well as some from other parts of Britain.

Oxford University does not exist as such. Each college is virtually autonomous, with its own rules and administration. It is the world-famous landmarks that form the real core of the University - the Radcliffe Camera, the Sheldonian Theatre, the Divinity School and the Bodleian Library among them. A stroll through the heart of Oxford illustrates the contrast between the quiet dignity of the colleges and these older foundations and the noise and bustle of the city streets.

Oxford has grown and evolved as a place of learning and a sumptuous treasure-house of medieval architecture thanks to the benevolence and generosity of some of the most powerful and influential figures of the day. William Morris, otherwise known as Viscount Nuffield, Bishop John Fell and Joseph Williamson, Secretary of State, were among them. In 1249, William of Durham left 310 marks to help support masters of arts studying theology, and in 1280 the University used what money was left to found University College, which now occupies a site in High Street, or the High as it is better known.

Two other colleges were founded prior to University College. During the second half of the 13th century, John Balliol founded the college which bears his name in Broad Street, and around the same time Walter de Merton, bishop and statesman, founded Merton College, famous for its cobbled roadway. Worcester College also dates from the 13th century. The trend for founding new colleges continued throughout the 14th and 15th centuries. By this time there was growing conflict in Oxford between 'town and gown' as charters bestowed upon the city from successive monarchs conveyed privileges to the University, which aggravated the city merchants. It was not until 1525 that Oxford could boast its finest and perhaps most famous college, Christ Church. Its great hall and magnificent art collection are an important part of any visitor's itinerary. The college chapel is the Cathedral Church of the Oxford Diocese.

Oxford includes five women's colleges which date from the end of the 19th century, and among the most modern colleges are St Catherine's and Wolfson, both founded during the post-war years. There are also several postgraduate colleges.

A stroll through Oxford's streets also reveals much about the city's role in the English Civil War. Oxford was the Royalist headquarters as well as the seat of Charles I's parliament. It was in St Giles that the King drilled his men, while the nearby Martyrs' Memorial, designed by Sir Gilbert Scott, recalls the burning at the stake of the Protestant martyrs, Ridley, Latimer and Cranmer, during the 16th century.

Oxford's rivers are an intrinsic part of the city's beauty and character. Folly Bridge provides memorable views of the Thames below and glimpses of the city beyond. The castellated Victorian house by the bridge survives as one of Oxford's best-known landmarks. The Thames and the Cherwell, pronounced 'Charwell', unite near here, with tree-shaded paths and sleepy backwaters offering delightful vistas across lush meadows to the honey-coloured stone of the college buildings.

and punts are available for hire at Folly Bridge, and here, too, there are river cruises downstream.

During the 20th century Oxford, like many towns and cities across the country, witnessed sweeping changes. The age of the motor car had been ushered in, and in 1913 William Morris built his first motorised vehicle in a

Christ Church Meadow is especially popular with visitors and local residents; and nearby Port Meadow, renowned for its vast expanse of open grazing land, has not changed since William the Conqueror presented it to the burgesses of Oxford as a free common. These damp meadows with their lush pastures attracted West Saxon farmers, and by the 5th century they had started to ford the Thames at nearby Hinksey. The Oxford stretch of Britain's greatest river comes to life during Eights Week in May, one of the city's brightest and most colourful occasions. Rowing boats

workshop at Cowley. By the late 1930s the car industry had made an enormous impact on Oxford, with new housing estates built to accommodate the thousands of people who worked at the plant.

There have been many other changes over the years, but at the start of the 21st century, Oxford still retains its elegance and grace. It remains a place of infinite beauty, beloved of dons and scholars, tourists and city dwellers. Above all, Oxford is synonymous with man's cultural heritage.

COWLEY 1890 26803

More than one hundred years ago Cowley was nothing more than a large village, its intricate maze of rooftops stretching towards the horizon. Today, the motor industry dominates this sprawling suburb of the city, and much of Cowley has changed beyond recognition.

THE PLAIN 1922 71998

Located on the east side of Magdalen Bridge, The Plain signifies the boundary of the old city. Just out of sight, the River Cherwell flows under the easterly part of the High Street. Close by is Magdalen College, the first building of any size and importance you pass on entering the city by the old London road.

FROM MAGDALEN TOWER 1890 26802
This view of Oxford's dreaming spires remains as impressive today as it was when this photograph was taken during the last years of Queen Victoria's reign. In the foreground is the city's famous High Street, often described as one of the most beautiful streets in Europe.

MAGDALEN COLLEGE AND THE RIVER CHERWELL c1950 033110

The college buildings have changed little since they were built at the end of the fifteenth century. The New Buildings, which date back to 1733, blend harmoniously with the older parts of the college; the hall has an impressive Jacobean screen and there are some valuable manuscripts in the library.

MAGDALEN COLLEGE 1890 26819

On May morning a famous Oxford tradition is upheld when the dons and the Magdalen College choristers gather at the top of the Perpendicular bell tower to sing a Latin hymn. This charming picture is enhanced by a delightful view of the Cherwell.

MAGDALEN COLLEGE FROM THE BRIDGE 1938   88122

MAGDALEN COLLEGE
from the Bridge 1938

The tower, marking the eastern entrance to the High Street, dates back to 1492 and took seventeen years to complete. The delay was probably caused by lengthy financial problems. During the Civil War Royalist forces defended the bridge here by hurling rocks from the top of the tower at the Parliamentarians assembled below.

◆

MAGDALEN COLLEGE BRIDGE 1922

This charming picture captures the atmosphere of 1920s Oxford. Punting on the Cherwell near Magdalen Bridge has long been a traditional summer activity for undergraduates and visitors to the city, though sometimes a paddle is preferable to a punt-pole.

MAGDALEN COLLEGE BRIDGE 1922   72007

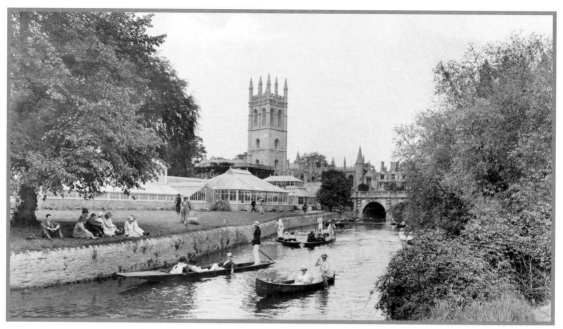

MAGDALEN COLLEGE FROM THE RIVER 1922 72005

Lying in the shadow of Magdalen Tower are the buildings of the University Botanic Garden, founded in 1621 by the Earl of Danby and established on the site of a 13th-century Jewish burial ground. More than 300 plants have been grown here for both teaching and research.

CHRIST CHURCH 1937 88112

At the beginning of the 15th century, the priory and church of St Frideswide were the main buildings on this site. It was in 1523 that Cardinal Wolsey, then the most powerful man in the country, decided to found a college at Oxford. Wolsey dissolved twenty-two monasteries to raise sufficient funds, sweeping away the priory and other buildings in the process.

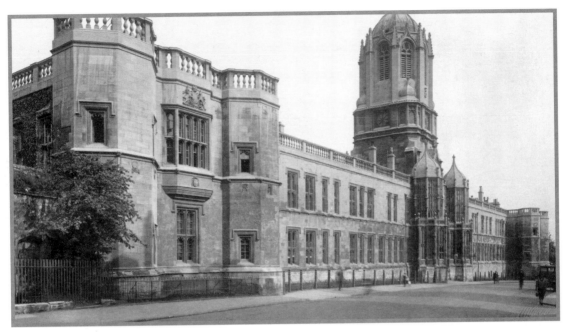

CHRIST CHURCH, WEST FRONT 1922   72010

Cardinal Wolsey had very ambitious plans for Christ Church. He wanted it to be much more than simply one college among many within the city. The size of the quadrangle, the hall and the kitchen give more than a hint of what he planned, but Wolsey fell from power before work could be completed.

CHRIST CHURCH 1890   26813

Robert Peel, William Gladstone and W H Auden were among the college's more distinguished students, and when John Fell was dean here, one of his scholars based a famous Latin epigram on him following a reprimand.

CHRIST CHURCH 1922 72009
The Cathedral's official title is The Cathedral Church of Christ in Oxford. It has a unique place in the history of Oxford. Not only is it the smallest of all English cathedrals, but it is also the college chapel of Christ Church.

CHRIST CHURCH, TOM TOWER 1890 26815
Tom Tower is such an integral feature of Oxford that it is synonymous with the city's world-famous skyline. Oxford simply would not be Oxford without it. John Fell, one-time Dean of Christ Church, engaged Christopher Wren to crown the main gateway with Tom Tower, transferring the medieval bell known as Old Tom from the cathedral to the college.

CHRIST CHURCH TOWER 1890 26829

Largely covered by creeper, Christ Church Tower dominates this striking Victorian photograph. Among other features, the college is renowned for its magnificent hall, impressive timbered roof and fine collection of portraits, including Henry VIII and Cardinal Wolsey.

PEMBROKE COLLEGE 1890 26882

The college was founded in 1624, and the front quadrangle was built between 1624 and 1670. William Morris, the renowned car manufacturer and philanthropist, gave benefactions to various colleges, including Pembroke. Dr Johnson was an undergraduate here, and the college is famous for its half-gallon teapot.

ST ALDATES c1950 033137

With international visitors and tourists thronging the streets, St Aldates is much busier today than it was when this photograph was taken. Christ Church, sometimes known as 'The House', can be seen on the right, with Wren's splendid creation, Tom Tower, rising above it.

ST ALDATES CHURCH 1890 26945

Originally a Saxon church, St Aldates was rebuilt in 1004. After the Dissolution of the Monasteries, it was acquired by the Crown before becoming part of Pembroke College. Its members worshipped here until the college built its own chapel in 1732.

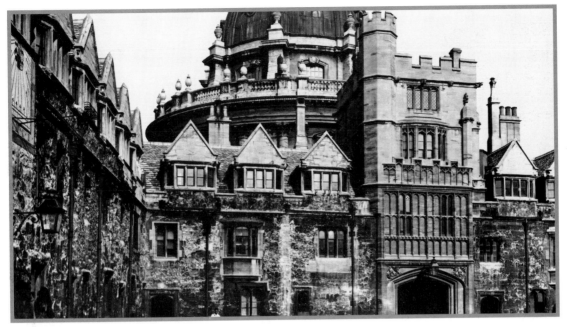

BRASENOSE COLLEGE QUADRANGLE 1890 26885
Founded early in the 16th century, Brasenose College takes its name from an ancient brass door knocker which, some sources suggest, was brought back here in 1890 after it had been removed by rebellious students to another college, Brasenose Hall, at Stamford in Lincolnshire.

QUEEN'S COLLEGE, THE FRONT QUADRANGLE 1890 26924
Neat manicured lawns unfold beneath the Hall and Chapel of Queen's College, crowned by a small but distinctive domed tower. Beneath it is a carved pediment decorated with symbolic figures of Justice, Neptune and Plenty.

HIGH STREET 1900 45181
On the right is the facade of Queen's College,
a glorious Grecian building designed by Sir Christopher
Wren's pupil, Hawksmoor. The first stone was laid in
1710 to coincide with the birthday of Queen Anne.

HIGH STREET 1922 71992
Queen's College dominates this fascinating photograph. Beneath the cupola above the central gateway is a statue of Caroline, Queen of George II, who donated £1,000 towards the completion of the quadrangle. Note the lady cyclists in their fashionable hats of the period.

HIGH STREET 1890 26912

Queen's College, named after Philippa, wife of Edward III, was originally founded to educate 'Poor Boys' from the north of England. However, one of those deprived scholars was the enterprising Joseph Williamson who later became Secretary of State. It was he who transformed Queen's into the college it is today.

HIGH STREET 1900 45182

St Mary the Virgin Church stands on the site of an 11th-century church which was once Oxford's most famous building. The present church includes a memorial to Dr John Radcliffe, one of the city's most distinguished sons. Note how quiet the street is compared with today's modern traffic.

HIGH STREET 1900 45183
Designed by Hawksmoor, the delicate spire of All Saints Church is a striking feature of the Oxford skyline. The church dates from the 18th century, replacing a Norman church which was destroyed when the spire fell on top of it. Today, All Saints is the library of Lincoln College.

HIGH STREET 1922 71989
Soaring above the High Street is the spire of St Mary the Virgin
Church, dating back to the 14th century. The even older tower is
13th-century. This impressive photograph highlights the contrast
between Oxford's distinguished architectural styles and the
modern cars and fashions of the 1920s.

HIGH STREET 1937 88069

When walking the street's length from east to west, you can appreciate the sweeping curve which gradually reveals some of Oxford's most striking landmarks. The dignified charm and distinguished architecture of its buildings sum up the beauty of this city.

ORIEL COLLEGE 1912 64076

The college was founded in 1326 by Adam de Brome, Almoner to King Edward II, who was its first Provost. Sir Walter Raleigh and Cecil Rhodes are among the more famous men associated with Oriel. The college was famously linked with the Oxford Movement, and Keble, Froude, Pusey and Thomas Arnold all became elected fellows.

JESUS COLLEGE, THE QUADRANGLE 1902   48623

Jesus College has long been synonymous with Wales. It was founded by Queen Elizabeth I in 1571 at the request of Hugh ap Rice, who endowed it and provided scholarships for Welsh students; the college chapel and library date back to the 17th century.

LINCOLN COLLEGE 1906   53698

Founded in 1427 by the Bishop of Lincoln, Lincoln College has a chequered history. Financial difficulties prevented the college from being completed: at the time of the Bishop's death in 1431, only the gate tower and staircase had been finished. The college's future looked bleak. However, various benefactors eventually came to the rescue, enabling the work to be completed.

LINCOLN COLLEGE 1927 79692
The magnificent hall is the oldest among the Oxford
colleges, with its impressive 15th-century timbered roof
still intact. Small and intimate, the hall is especially
attractive when fellows and students dine by candlelight.

ST GILES' STREET 1890 26914
Partly visible on the left of this photograph is Oxford's
Taylor Institute, dedicated to the study of modern
languages at the University. Statues symbolising the
Romance languages of France, Italy, Germany and
Spain adorn the front of this splendid building, which
was founded with a bequest from an 18th-century
architect, Sir Robert Taylor.

ST GILES c1950 033112

It was here in St Giles that Charles I drilled his men during the Civil War. Over on the left, screened by trees, is one of Oxford's most famous hostelries, The Eagle and Child. J R R Tolkien, C S Lewis, Charles Williams and other dons met here every Tuesday morning between 1939 and 1962.

KEBLE COLLEGE 1890 26853

One of Oxford's most striking buildings, Keble is characterized by its red and blackish-blue brick, polychrome patterns, bands, chequers, trellises and buff stone. Its exuberant design dazzles the eye. The college, designed by William Butterfield, was established in 1870 as a memorial to John Keble, where young men of limited means could be taught under the influence of the Church of England.

St John's College 1900 45188

This turn-of-the-century photograph depicts the Canterbury Quadrangle, famous for its two loggias and two libraries. The quadrangle was almost entirely created by Archbishop Laud. St John's was founded in 1555 and is noted for its fine gardens.

Balliol College 1890 26905

A clock peeps into view high above the quadrangle of Balliol College, one of Oxford's three oldest colleges. Former prime ministers Edward Heath and Harold Macmillan were students here, as were Matthew Arnold and Graham Greene. The college was founded by John de Balliol.

BALLIOL COLLEGE 1922 72017

'It is fitting that Balliol, the most progressive of our colleges, should have so large a proportion of its buildings modern', wrote Dr Wells in 1897. Up until the early 19th century, Balliol's reputation was flawed, and the college was dismissed as 'a dear, dim drinking college'. Open scholarships and clever tutors helped transform Balliol's image.

SHIP STREET AND EXETER COLLEGE CHAPEL 1922 72050

Exeter College was founded by one of Exeter's bishops in 1314, though most of the college buildings have been restored or rebuilt over the years. The Victorian chapel was designed by Sir Gilbert Scott, and includes various tapestries by Burne-Jones and William Morris. Note Ye Olde North Gate Teahouse on the corner.

ALL SOULS COLLEGE AND THE RADCLIFFE CAMERA 1890   26859

Founded in 1437 by Henry Chichele to commemorate Henry V and those who fell at Agincourt, All Souls is distinguished by some of the finest architecture in Oxford. The tower displaying the college arms was designed by Hawksmoor. The Radcliffe Camera is one of the reading rooms for the Bodleian Library, its dome an outstanding landmark on the city's skyline.

THE RADCLIFFE CAMERA 1937   88079

Designed by James Gibbs and completed in 1749, the Radcliffe Camera was paid for by a bequest from John Radcliffe, and originally housed a collection of books provided by him. The principal chamber under the dome is where undergraduates come regularly to read and study.

BROAD STREET 1897   40021
Broad Street is famous throughout Oxford for its
assortment of bookshops. Two of the city's most
notable colleges, Trinity and Balliol, line the left-hand
side of the street, while the striking facade of the
Clarendon Building can be seen at the far end. Note
the ornately designed street lamp in the centre.

BROAD STREET 1890 26942

Over to the right is the unmistakable facade of the Sheldonian Theatre, designed by Christopher Wren and opened in 1669. Built for meetings and concerts, the theatre was named after Gilbert Sheldon, the 17th-century Archbishop of Canterbury. To the left of it is the Clarendon Building, formerly the headquarters of the Oxford University Press.

THE SHELDONIAN THEATRE 1922 72026

Designed by Sir Christopher Wren, and planned like a Roman theatre, the Sheldonian was his first major work on this scale. Opened on 9 July 1669, the theatre was named after its benefactor, Archbishop Sheldon. University books were printed here in the 17th century.

NEW COLLEGE
The Entrance Gateway 1902

The college, founded in 1379 by William of Wykeham, lies in the shadow of the old city wall. The gatehouse was where the Warden monitored the activities of his students. New College has one of the oldest quadrangles in Oxford.

NEW COLLEGE 1890

Many of the original college buildings are in the Perpendicular style, and survive as a permanent reminder of Wykeham's design. The cloisters and the chapel, the latter restored by James Wyatt and Gilbert Scott, are particularly striking. The connection between the college and Winchester School is still maintained today.

NEW COLLEGE, THE ENTRANCE GATEWAY 1902   48626

NEW COLLEGE 1890   26889

49

BATH PLACE 1926 79312

BATH PLACE 1926

Away from the city streets and colleges, visitors can stumble upon Oxford's hidden corners and sleepy backwaters. Bath Place, off Holywell Street, is just such a place. Its Victorian, Georgian and timber-framed buildings give it a fascinating mix of architectural styles.

◆

ST PETER'S IN THE EAST 1890

One of the city's lesser-known buildings, St Peter's in the East is a wonderful old church which lies hidden in the shadow of St Edmund Hall. The church, which includes a vaulted Norman crypt beneath the chancel, is close to New College Garden.

ST PETER'S IN THE EAST 1890 26946

HERTFORD COLLEGE 1906 53700

Dating back to 1284, Hertford College had fallen into decay by the middle of the 19th century, though its fortunes were later revived by Act of Parliament. The college was founded as Hart Hall, and stands on the site of several previous halls.

HERTFORD COLLEGE BRIDGE 1922 72025

Another of Oxford's much-loved landmarks is the Hertford College Bridge, or the Bridge of Sighs as it is otherwise known. This outstanding structure, which dates back to the beginning of the First World War and is a replica of its Venice namesake, connects the north and south quadrangles of Hertford College.

SOMERVILLE COLLEGE 1907 57393
Named after Mary Somerville, a Scottish mathematician, Somerville College boasts two prime ministers among its graduates - Indira Gandhi and Margaret Thatcher. Vera Brittain and the writer Dorothy L Sayers were also students at Somerville. Much of the college is hidden from the street.

SOMERVILLE COLLEGE 1907 57394
It was in 1878 that the Association for Promoting the Higher Education of Women proposed to found a hall in Oxford for women students. The hall opened the following year with 12 students - initially as Somerville Hall, then from 1886 as Somerville College.

WADHAM COLLEGE 1902 48628
Sir Christopher Wren attended Wadham College, and the clock in the quadrangle was designed by him. The college itself was planned by Nicholas Wadham, and it was completed four years after his death. The chapel and hall are particularly striking.

FROM CARFAX TOWER 1922 71988
At the centre of this impressive rooftop photograph of Oxford is the city's splendid Town Hall building, an architectural treasure both inside and out. Queen Street lies at the bottom of the picture and is named after Queen Charlotte, wife of George III.

FROM CARFAX TOWER 1922   71986
Breathtaking views of Oxford are captured in this photograph of the city taken from the top of
Carfax Tower. Among the most prominent landmarks are the Radcliffe Camera and the spire of
All Saints Church. Down below to the right are the premises of Wyatt and Sons, Drapers and
Milliners, as advertised on the awning.

CARFAX TOWER 1922 71997
A policeman directs traffic in this city centre photograph. It is here at Carfax that four busy streets meet. Carfax Tower is where Charles II was proclaimed King in May 1660. The clock is famous for its quarter-boys, which strike every fifteen minutes.

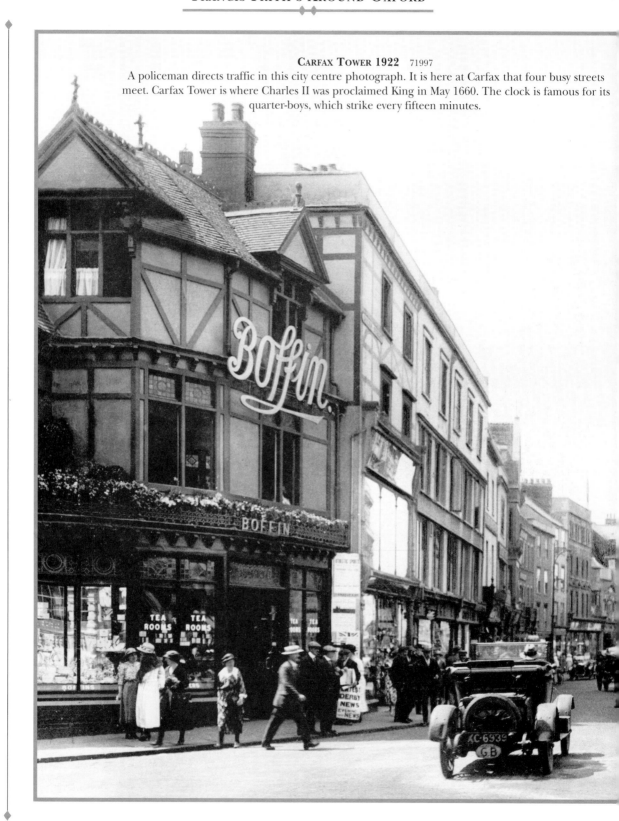

THE CARFAX 1937 88074

Over on the left there used to be a 'pennyless bench', where women sold butter and beggars scrounged a few shillings from passers-by. More than 300 years before this photograph was taken, the Carfax Conduit was built in the middle of the junction, conveying piped water from nearby Hinksey.

CORNMARKET STREET 1922 71994

The London, City & Midland Bank can be seen on the corner of busy Cornmarket and Carfax. Note the signs attached to the lamp standard, pointing to London and Gloucester. The awning of H Samuel, jeweller, is clearly visible on the right.

CORNMARKET STREET 1922 71995

St Michael's Church, where John Wesley preached from the 15th-century pulpit in 1726, is just visible further along the street. The Saxon tower is the oldest surviving building in Oxford. The Clarendon Hotel ceased trading many years ago.

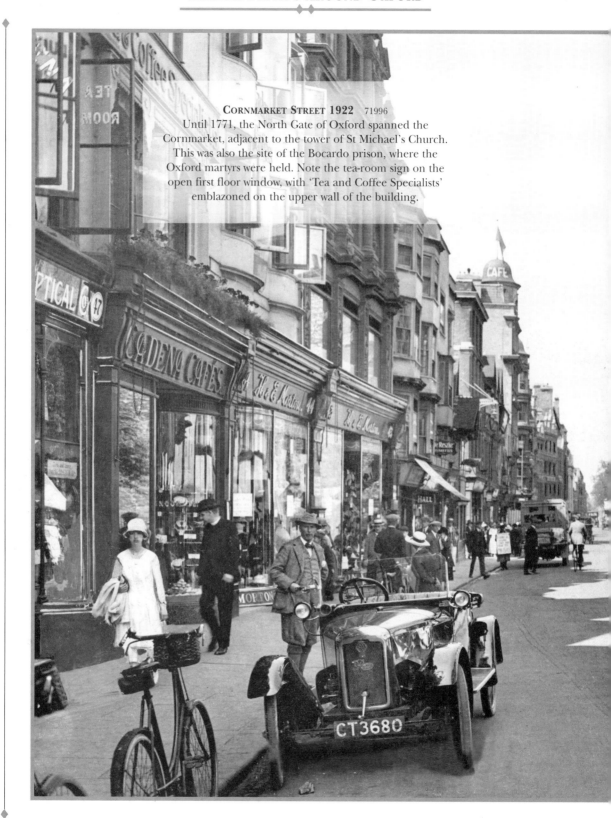

CORNMARKET STREET 1922 71996
Until 1771, the North Gate of Oxford spanned the
Cornmarket, adjacent to the tower of St Michael's Church.
This was also the site of the Bocardo prison, where the
Oxford martyrs were held. Note the tea-room sign on the
open first floor window, with 'Tea and Coffee Specialists'
emblazoned on the upper wall of the building.

CORNMARKET STREET c1950 O33129
The breathtaking outline of Tom Tower dominates St Aldates on the far side of Carfax. Morris Garages and the premises of Barclays Bank are on the right. Note that there are several cyclists in the picture; the number of bicycles in Oxford has grown dramatically in recent years.

QUEEN'S STREET c1950 O33124
Until it was demolished at the end of the 19th century, St Martin's Church stood on this site. The heavily-restored medieval church tower is all that is left of St Martin's, which was known as the city church; it was a focal point and meeting place in times of war or victory.

THE DIVINITY SCHOOL 1907

Built to provide a theological lecture room, the Divinity School dates back to 1427-80. The photograph depicts the school's magnificent vaulted roof, which consists of four arches and is beautifully decorated with figures and coats of arms. It was once used as a corn store before being renovated by Wren.

THE UNION CLUB 1890

Dating back to the Victorian and Edwardian eras, the Oxford Union consists of various buildings in the style of the Gothic Revival. William Morris, who, among others, painted the library frescoes, is said to have dined at Christ Church, his hair splattered with blue paint.

THE DIVINITY SCHOOL 1907   57372

THE UNION CLUB 1890   26943

THE CASTLE 1912 64171

At the centre of this photograph lies the Norman tower of Oxford Castle. Within its precincts lie a Saxon mound and a Norman crypt. The castle overlooks a branch of the river where it meanders between run-down buildings and small factories.

THE RIVER FROM FOLLY BRIDGE 1890 26948

This Victorian photograph was taken from Folly Bridge, which originally had a tower and gatehouse and was used by Roger Bacon, the 13th-century astronomer and scientist, as an observatory. In addition to Folly Bridge, Bacon also used the tower of Sunningwell Church near Abingdon.

THE UNIVERSITY BARGES 1890 26949

It is difficult to imagine Oxford without the Thames. It is this great river that helps to make the city what it is. The Romans called the Thames Thamesis, but where the Thames becomes the Isis and the Isis becomes the Thames again is not clear.

THE EIGHTS 1922 72059

The Thames is not sufficiently wide at Oxford for the conventional kind of race in which one boat, known as an eight, overtakes another. The broad, sweeping movements of the oars requires a lot of space. Instead, the crews begin the race in line before trying to outmanoeuvre the one in front by bumping it.

THE EIGHTS 1922 72063
One of the most colourful events on the Thames, Eights
Week takes place in May: it is then that the college barges
and the river banks rapidly fill up with riverside spectators
and those who simply enjoy the social aspect of the occasion.

THE EIGHTS 1906 53695

This photograph was taken from Folly Bridge; the reach from here to Iffley Lock is used by the college eights for training, and for the bump races known as Torpids and Eights. This stretch of the Thames is known as Isis; near here it meets its tributary, the River Cherwell.

THE EIGHTS 1922 72061

The object of Eights Week is for each crew to move up one place in a complex table of positions maintained from year to year. Each year every boat starts off in the position it occupied from the previous year in the table. The position of head of the river and the second, third and fourth places are the most coveted.

ON THE RIVER 1922 72056

This scenic stretch of the Thames, overlooked by Christ Church Meadow, has long been a rowing reach; at one time the bank would have been lined with eye-catching college barges, which were used as grandstands and clubhouses. Many of them have now gone - fallen into decay or converted into modest houseboats or holiday accommodation.

THE COLLEGE BARGES 1922   72051

During the 1920s, colourful college barges lined the north bank of the river as far as the eye could see. The barges were considered ideal for socialising and witnessing Eights Week in May. Today, smaller and more practical forms of river craft can be seen moored along the riverside.

ON THE CHERWELL 1912 64172

Hemmed in by a circle of hills and built on a gravel bank between the Thames Isis and the River Cherwell, Oxford creates the impression of sitting on an island. It was the damp climate here which probably drove the Romans away.

THE ROLLERS, ON THE CHERWELL 1922 72066

A charming picture showing plenty of colourful punting activity on the Cherwell. The tree-shaded riverside path has long been a popular shortcut linking the Thames riverbank with the High Street and Magdalen Bridge.

VIEW ON THE CHERWELL 1906 53704
Like the Thames, the Cherwell has long been a popular river for boating, punting, fishing and bathing.
Pronounced Charwell, the quiet, placid river forms the eastern boundary of the University Parks. A path runs
along the east bank, reached by the high-arched Rainbow footbridge.

VIEW ON THE CHERWELL 1906 53705

Here on this tributary of the Thames visitors, locals and sightseers stroll undisturbed and yet remain in the shadow of the city. Wordsworth was greatly inspired by the classic view of Christ Church Meadow, beyond which are Oxford's magnificent spires and college buildings.

ADDISON'S WALK 1937 88125

The tree-shaded Magdalen Walks along the bank of the Cherwell are truly delightful and a perfect way to study the changing seasons. Addison's Walk is dedicated to the memory of Joseph Addison, who was a fellow of Magdalen College.

MARSTON FERRY 1912 64174
Children cross the river at Marston, once a village but now a north Oxford suburb. During the Civil War, the old manor house was the headquarters of the Parliamentarian army. A cannon-ball fired from here struck the north wall of Christ Church, where Charles I and his court were staying at the time.

CUDDESDON, THE OLD MILL AND THE RIVER c1955 C292021
The 18th-century working water-mill lies on the River Thame, about a mile from the centre of the village of Cuddesdon. This photograph perfectly captures the peace and rural tranquillity of the scene. The Thame flows into the Thames at Dorchester, a few miles to the south.

CUDDESDON, HIGH STREET c1955   C292009

Cuddesdon was once the home of the Bishops of Oxford. There was a palace here, set ablaze in 1644 to prevent the Parliamentary troops in the Civil War from seizing it. A new palace was built by Bishop Fell in 1679. Bishop Bancroft, the founder of the original palace, is buried in the churchyard.

CUDDESDON
High Street c1955
This photograph shows Cuddesdon's long High Street, with the pub sign just visible at the far end. The village, on the eastern side of Garsington Hill, to the east of Oxford, boasts many stone-built houses and picturesque cottages.

◆

CUDDESDON
Denton Hill c1955
Denton Hill is part of Cuddesdon. The name of the village is Saxon and means 'hill of Cuthwine.' From the churchyard there are wonderful views across the plain of Oxford to the Chilterns beyond.

CUDDESDON, HIGH STREET c1955 C292014

CUDDESDON, DENTON HILL c1955 C292006

CUDDESDON, CUDDESDON COLLEGE c1955 C292010

Cuddesdon Theological College was founded by Bishop Wilberforce and opened in June 1854. The college was designed by George Street, the distinguished Victorian architect; he was also responsible for the Law Courts, and the style is neo-Gothic with a Decorated chapel.

SANDFORD-ON-THAMES, THE LOCK c1955 S348012

The Thames divides into two here, with several weirs and a lock. There was once a Victorian mill here, though that has now been replaced by housing. Nearby is the site of a Knights Templar hospice founded in 1274.

SANDFORD-ON-THAMES, THE LOCK c1955 S348009

South of Iffley the Thames makes for Sandford. The lock here has the greatest fall of water on the river, with the water from adjacent Sandford Pool thundering over the weir, which is known as the Sandford Lasher. The Lasher has claimed several lives over the years.

SANDFORD-ON-THAMES, THE RIVER AND THE KINGS ARMS HOTEL c1955 S348004

The Kings Arms is 15th-century; much of the building was once part of a thriving paper-mill. This photograph recalls the days when the mill was still in use, and the chimney was something of a local landmark. A ferry service operated from here as early as the 13th century.

SANDFORD-ON-THAMES, ST ANDREW'S CHURCH c1955   S348003

Not much remains of the Early Norman church founded here at the end of the 11th century. Note the church porch, which was restored by Dame Eliza Isham in 1652 and bears the inscription: 'Thanks to thy charitie religious dame, which found me old and made me new againe.'

SANDFORD-ON-THAMES, THE MAIN ROAD c1955   S348011

The village is situated on a loop of the Thames between Oxford and Abingdon. Today, Sandford is a rapidly-expanding riverside village, but in the 1950s, it was a quiet rural community. Note the old RAC logo on the left.

WYTHAM, THE VILLAGE c1965   W259301

Pronounced 'white'em', this is one of Oxfordshire's prettiest villages. Plenty of stone-built houses and cottages stand in the shadow of Wytham Great Wood, and just to the south lies 700-acre Wytham Park. The house is now part of Oxford University. Note the White Hart pub sign on the corner.

WYTHAM, THE CHURCH c1965   W259302

The original church dates back to about 1480; it is thought to have been built by the monks of Abingdon Abbey. It was completely rebuilt in 1811 with various materials from Cumnor Place, which was destroyed by the third Earl of Abingdon.

Index

Frith Book Co Titles

www.francisfrith.co.uk

The Frith Book Company publishes over 100 new titles each year. A selection of those currently available are listed below. For latest catalogue please contact Frith Book Co.

Town Books 96pages, approx 100 photos. County and Themed Books 128pages, approx 150 photos (unless specified). All titles hardback laminated case and jacket except those indicated pb (paperback)

Ancient Monuments & Stone Circles	1-85937-143-4	£17.99
Aylesbury (pb)	1-85937-227-9	£9.99
Bakewell	1-85937-113-2	£12.99
Barnstaple (pb)	1-85937-300-3	£9.99
Bath	1-85937-097-7	£12.99
Bedford (pb)	1-85937-205-8	£9.99
Berkshire (pb)	1-85937-191-4	£9.99
Berkshire Churches	1-85937-170-1	£17.99
Bognor Regis (pb)	1-85937-431-x	£9.99
Bournemouth	1-85937-067-5	£12.99
Bradford (pb)	1-85937-204-x	£9.99
Brighton & Hove(pb)	1-85937-192-2	£8.99
Bristol (pb)	1-85937-264-3	£9.99
British Life A Century Ago (pb)	1-85937-213-9	£9.99
Buckinghamshire (pb)	1-85937-200-7	£9.99
Camberley (pb)	1-85937-222-8	£9.99
Cambridge (pb)	1-85937-422-0	£9.99
Cambridgeshire (pb)	1-85937-420-4	£9.99
Canals & Waterways (pb)	1-85937-291-0	£9.99
Canterbury Cathedral (pb)	1-85937-179-5	£9.99
Cardiff (pb)	1-85937-093-4	£9.99
Carmarthenshire	1-85937-216-3	£14.99
Cheltenham (pb)	1-85937-095-0	£9.99
Cheshire (pb)	1-85937-271-6	£9.99
Chester	1-85937-090-x	£12.99
Chesterfield	1-85937-071-3	£9.99
Chichester (pb)	1-85937-228-7	£9.99
Colchester (pb)	1-85937-188-4	£8.99
Cornish Coast	1-85937-163-9	£14.99
Cornwall (pb)	1-85937-229-5	£9.99
Cornwall Living Memories	1-85937-248-1	£14.99
Cotswolds (pb)	1-85937-230-9	£9.99
Cotswolds Living Memories	1-85937-255-4	£14.99
County Durham	1-85937-123-x	£14.99
Cumbria	1-85937-101-9	£14.99
Dartmoor	1-85937-145-0	£14.99
Derbyshire (pb)	1-85937-196-5	£9.99
Devon (pb)	1-85937-297-x	£9.99
Dorset (pb)	1-85937-269-4	£9.99
Dorset Churches	1-85937-172-8	£17.99
Dorset Coast (pb)	1-85937-299-6	£9.99

Dorset Living Memories	1-85937-210-4	£14.99
Down the Severn	1-85937-118-3	£14.99
Down the Thames (pb)	1-85937-278-3	£9.99
Dublin (pb)	1-85937-231-7	£9.99
East Anglia (pb)	1-85937-265-1	£9.99
East London	1-85937-080-2	£14.99
East Sussex	1-85937-130-2	£14.99
Eastbourne	1-85937-061-6	£12.99
Edinburgh (pb)	1-85937-193-0	£8.99
English Castles (pb)	1-85937-434-4	£9.99
English Country Houses	1-85937-161-2	£17.99
Exeter	1-85937-126-4	£12.99
Exmoor	1-85937-132-9	£14.99
Falmouth	1-85937-066-7	£12.99
Folkestone (pb)	1-85937-124-8	£9.99
Glasgow (pb)	1-85937-190-6	£9.99
Gloucestershire	1-85937-102-7	£14.99
Greater Manchester (pb)	1-85937-266-x	£9.99
Hampshire Churches (pb)	1-85937-207-4	£9.99
Harrogate	1-85937-423-9	£9.99
Hastings & Bexhill (pb)	1-85937-131-0	£9.99
Heart of Lancashire (pb)	1-85937-197-3	£9.99
Helston (pb)	1-85937-214-7	£9.99
Hereford (pb)	1-85937-175-2	£9.99
Herefordshire	1-85937-174-4	£14.99
Humberside	1-85937-215-5	£14.99
Hythe, Romney Marsh & Ashford	1-85937-256-2	£9.99
Ipswich (pb)	1-85937-424-7	£9.99
Ireland (pb)	1-85937-181-7	£9.99
Isles of Scilly	1-85937-136-1	£14.99
Isle of Wight (pb)	1-85937-429-8	£9.99
Isle of Wight Living Memories	1-85937-304-6	£14.99
Kent (pb)	1-85937-189-2	£9.99
Kent Living Memories	1-85937-125-6	£14.99
Lake District (pb)	1-85937-275-9	£9.99
Lancaster, Morecambe & Heysham (pb)	1-85937-233-3	£9.99
Leeds (pb)	1-85937-202-3	£9.99
Leicester	1-85937-073-x	£12.99
Leicestershire (pb)	1-85937-185-x	£9.99
Lighthouses	1-85937-257-0	£17.99
Lincolnshire (pb)	1-85937-433-6	£9.99

Available from your local bookshop or from the publisher

Frith Book Co Titles (continued)

Liverpool & Merseyside (pb)	1-85937-234-1	£9.99	Southampton (pb)	1-85937-427-1	£9.99
London (pb)	1-85937-183-3	£9.99	Southport (pb)	1-85937-425-5	£9.99
Ludlow (pb)	1-85937-176-0	£9.99	Stratford upon Avon	1-85937-098-5	£12.99
Luton (pb)	1-85937-235-x	£9.99	Suffolk (pb)	1-85937-221-x	£9.99
Manchester (pb)	1-85937-198-1	£9.99	Suffolk Coast	1-85937-259-7	£14.99
New Forest	1-85937-128-0	£14.99	Surrey (pb)	1-85937-240-6	£9.99
Newport, Wales (pb)	1-85937-258-9	£9.99	Sussex (pb)	1-85937-184-1	£9.99
Newquay (pb)	1-85937-421-2	£9.99	Swansea (pb)	1-85937-167-1	£9.99
Norfolk (pb)	1-85937-195-7	£9.99	Tees Valley & Cleveland	1-85937-211-2	£14.99
Norfolk Living Memories	1-85937-217-1	£14.99	Thanet (pb)	1-85937-116-7	£9.99
Northamptonshire	1-85937-150-7	£14.99	Tiverton (pb)	1-85937-178-7	£9.99
Northumberland Tyne & Wear (pb)	1-85937-281-3	£9.99	Torbay	1-85937-063-2	£12.99
North Devon Coast	1-85937-146-9	£14.99	Truro	1-85937-147-7	£12.99
North Devon Living Memories	1-85937-261-9	£14.99	Victorian and Edwardian Cornwall	1-85937-252-x	£14.99
North Wales (pb)	1-85937-298-8	£9.99	Victorian & Edwardian Devon	1-85937-253-8	£14.99
North Yorkshire (pb)	1-85937-236-8	£9.99	Victorian & Edwardian Kent	1-85937-149-3	£14.99
Norwich (pb)	1-85937-194-9	£8.99	Vic & Ed Maritime Album	1-85937-144-2	£17.99
Nottingham (pb)	1-85937-324-0	£9.99	Victorian and Edwardian Sussex	1-85937-157-4	£14.99
Nottinghamshire (pb)	1-85937-187-6	£9.99	Victorian & Edwardian Yorkshire	1-85937-154-x	£14.99
Peak District (pb)	1-85937-280-5	£9.99	Victorian Seaside	1-85937-159-0	£17.99
Penzance	1-85937-069-1	£12.99	Villages of Devon (pb)	1-85937-293-7	£9.99
Peterborough (pb)	1-85937-219-8	£9.99	Villages of Kent (pb)	1-85937-294-5	£9.99
Piers	1-85937-237-6	£17.99	Warwickshire (pb)	1-85937-203-1	£9.99
Plymouth	1-85937-119-1	£12.99	Welsh Castles (pb)	1-85937-322-4	£9.99
Poole & Sandbanks (pb)	1-85937-251-1	£9.99	West Midlands (pb)	1-85937-289-9	£9.99
Preston (pb)	1-85937-212-0	£9.99	West Sussex	1-85937-148-5	£14.99
Reading (pb)	1-85937-238-4	£9.99	West Yorkshire (pb)	1-85937-201-5	£9.99
Salisbury (pb)	1-85937-239-2	£9.99	Weymouth (pb)	1-85937-209-0	£9.99
St Ives	1-85937-068-3	£12.99	Wiltshire (pb)	1-85937-277-5	£9.99
Scotland (pb)	1-85937-182-5	£9.99	Wiltshire Churches (pb)	1-85937-171-x	£9.99
Scottish Castles (pb)	1-85937-323-2	£9.99	Wiltshire Living Memories	1-85937-245-7	£14.99
Sheffield, South Yorks (pb)	1-85937-267-8	£9.99	Winchester (pb)	1-85937-428-x	£9.99
Shrewsbury (pb)	1-85937-325-9	£9.99	Windmills & Watermills	1-85937-242-2	£17.99
Shropshire (pb)	1-85937-326-7	£9.99	Worcestershire	1-85937-152-3	£14.99
Somerset	1-85937-153-1	£14.99	York (pb)	1-85937-199-x	£9.99
South Devon Coast	1-85937-107-8	£14.99	Yorkshire (pb)	1-85937-186-8	£9.99
South Devon Living Memories	1-85937-168-x	£14.99	Yorkshire Living Memories	1-85937-166-3	£14.99
South Hams	1-85937-220-1	£14.99			

Frith Book Co titles available soon

1880's England	Oct 01	1-85937-331-3	£17.99	Gloucester (pb)	Oct 01	1-85937-417-4	£9.99
Amersham & Chesham (pb)	Oct 01	1-85937-340-2	£9.99	Oxfordshire (pb)	Oct 01	1-85937-430-1	£9.99
Bedfordshire	Oct 01	1-85937-320-8	£14.99	Picturesque Harbours	Oct 01	1-85937-208-2	£17.99
Belfast (pb)	Oct 01	1-85937-303-8	£9.99	Romford (pb)	Oct 01	1-85937-319-4	£9.99
Britain Living Memories	Oct 01	1-85937-343-7	£17.99	Worcester (pb)	Oct 01	1-85937-165-5	£9.99
Chelmsford (pb)	Oct 01	1-85937-310-0	£9.99	Villages of Sussex (pb)	Oct 01	1-85937-295-3	£9.99

See Frith books on the internet www.francisfrith.co.uk

FRITH PRODUCTS & SERVICES

Francis Frith would doubtless be pleased to know that the pioneering publishing venture he started in 1860 still continues today. A hundred and forty years later, The Francis Frith Collection continues in the same innovative tradition and is now one of the foremost publishers of vintage photographs in the world. Some of the current activities include:

Interior Decoration

Today Frith's photographs can be seen framed and as giant wall murals in thousands of pubs, restaurants, hotels, banks, retail stores and other public buildings throughout the country. In every case they enhance the unique local atmosphere of the places they depict and provide reminders of gentler days in an increasingly busy and frenetic world.

Product Promotions

Frith products are used by many major companies to promote the sales of their own products or to reinforce their own history and heritage. Frith promotions have been used by Hovis bread, Courage beers, Scots Porage Oats, Colman's mustard, Cadbury's foods, Mellow Birds coffee, Dunhill pipe tobacco, Guinness, and Bulmer's Cider.

Genealogy and Family History

As the interest in family history and roots grows world-wide, more and more people are turning to Frith's photographs of Great Britain for images of the towns, villages and streets where their ancestors lived; and, of course, photographs of the churches and chapels where their ancestors were christened, married and buried are an essential part of every genealogy tree and family album.

Frith Products

All Frith photographs are available Framed or just as Mounted Prints and Posters (size 23 x 16 inches). These may be ordered from the address below. From time to time other products - Address Books, Calendars, Table Mats, etc - are available.

The Internet

Already twenty thousand Frith photographs can be viewed and purchased on the internet through the Frith websites and a myriad of partner sites.

For more detailed information on Frith companies and products, look at these sites:

www.francisfrith.co.uk
www.francisfrith.com
(for North American visitors)

See the complete list of Frith Books at:
www.francisfrith.co.uk

This web site is regularly updated with the latest list of publications from the Frith Book Company. If you wish to buy books relating to another part of the country that your local bookshop does not stock, you may purchase on-line.

For further information, trade, or author enquiries please contact us at the address below:
The Francis Frith Collection, Frith's Barn, Teffont, Salisbury, Wiltshire, England SP3 5QP.
Tel: +44 (0)1722 716 376 Fax: +44 (0)1722 716 881   Email: sales@francisfrith.co.uk

See Frith books on the internet www.francisfrith.co.uk

TO RECEIVE YOUR **FREE** MOUNTED PRINT

Mounted Print
Overall size 14 x 11 inches

Cut out this Voucher and return it with your remittance for £1.95 to cover postage and handling, to UK addresses. For overseas addresses please include £4.00 post and handling. Choose any photograph included in this book. Your SEPIA print will be A4 in size, and mounted in a cream mount with burgundy rule line, overall size 14 x 11 inches.

Order additional Mounted Prints at HALF PRICE (only £7.49 each*)

If there are further pictures you would like to order, possibly as gifts for friends and family, purchase them at half price (no additional postage and handling required).

Have your Mounted Prints framed*

For an additional £14.95 per print you can have your chosen Mounted Print framed in an elegant polished wood and gilt moulding, overall size 16 x 13 inches (no additional postage and handling required).

> *** IMPORTANT!**
> These special prices are only available if ordered using the original voucher on this page (no copies permitted) and at the same time as your free Mounted Print, for delivery to the same address

Frith Collectors' Guild

From time to time we publish a magazine of news and stories about Frith photographs and further special offers of Frith products. If you would like 12 months FREE membership, please return this form.

Send completed forms to:
The Francis Frith Collection, Frith's Barn, Teffont, Salisbury, Wiltshire SP3 5QP

Voucher for **FREE** and Reduced Price Frith Prints

Picture no.	Page number	Qty	Mounted @ £7.49	Framed + £14.95	Total Cost
		1	**Free of charge***	£	£
			£7.49	£	£
			£7.49	£	£
			£7.49	£	£
			£7.49	£	£
			£7.49	£	£

Please allow 28 days for delivery	*** Post & handling**	**£1.95**
Book Title	**Total Order Cost**	**£**

Please do not photocopy this voucher. Only the original is valid, so please cut it out and return it to us.

I enclose a cheque / postal order for £ . . . . made payable to 'The Francis Frith Collection' OR please debit my Mastercard / Visa / Switch / Amex card *(credit cards please on all overseas orders)*

Number . . . .

Issue No(Switch only) . . . . .Valid from (Amex/Switch) . . . .

Expires . . . .   Signature . . . .

Name Mr/Mrs/Ms . . . .

Address . . . .

. . . .

. . . .

. . . . Postcode . . . .

Daytime Tel No . . . .   Valid to 31/12/02

The Francis Frith Collectors' Guild

Please enrol me as a member for 12 months free of charge.

Name Mr/Mrs/Ms . . . .

Address . . . .

. . . .

. . . .

. . . . Postcode . . . .

Would you like to find out more about Francis Frith?

We have recently recruited some entertaining speakers who are happy to visit local groups, clubs and societies to give an illustrated talk documenting Frith's travels and photographs. If you are a member of such a group and are interested in hosting a presentation, we would love to hear from you.

Our speakers bring with them a small selection of our local town and county books, together with sample prints. They are happy to take orders. A small proportion of the order value is donated to the group who have hosted the presentation. The talks are therefore an excellent way of fundraising for small groups and societies.

Can you help us with information about any of the Frith photographs in this book?

We are gradually compiling an historical record for each of the photographs in the Frith archive. It is always fascinating to find out the names of the people shown in the pictures, as well as insights into the shops, buildings and other features depicted.

If you recognize anyone in the photographs in this book, or if you have information not already included in the author's caption, do let us know. We would love to hear from you, and will try to publish it in future books or articles.

Our production team

Frith books are produced by a small dedicated team at offices in the converted Grade II listed 18th-century barn at Teffont near Salisbury, illustrated above. Most have worked with the Frith Collection for many years. All have in common one quality: they have a passion for the Frith Collection. The team is constantly expanding, but currently includes:

Jason Buck, John Buck, Heather Crisp, Isobel Hall, Rob Hames, Hazel Heaton, Peter Horne, James Kinnear, Tina Leary, Eliza Sackett, Terence Sackett, Sandra Sanger, Shelley Tolcher, Susanna Walker, Clive Wathen, Jenny Wathen and Douglas Burns.